Be Careful Little Eyes

Helping Young Children Cope with Bad Pictures

Unless otherwise noted, Scripture quotations are from
The Holy Bible King James Version

Library of Congress Cataloging-in-Publication Data

Shivers, Frank R., 1949-
Be Careful Little Eyes / Frank Shivers
ISBN 9781878127419

Library of Congress Control Number:
2019905603

Illustrated by
Lisa Sizemore

For Information:
Frank Shivers Evangelistic Association
P. O. Box 9991
Columbia, South Carolina 29290
www.frankshivers.com

Presented To

_____

By

_____

Date

_____

"I will set no wicked [ugly, bad] thing before my eyes."
~ Psalm 101:3 AKJV

This book is dedicated to

Dave Walton

An exemplary example in soul winning at home and abroad and a defender of children and youth against the poison of pornography, alcohol and drugs.

JESUS

YOU

Contents

Preface

A personal word to parents.

"The eye is the lamp of the body. If your eyes are healthy, your whole body will be full of light. But if your eyes are unhealthy, your whole body will be full of darkness" (Matthew 6:22–23 NIV).

Some parents are like the mother that said she didn't want her child even to know the word *pornography*. I understand. As a grandfather, I wish my grands would never hear the word, much less its meaning. But that's not the world in which we live, is it? Sadly, it isn't—nor ever will be. It is, therefore, needful to be proactive in protecting children from its erotic and deviant material.

Prior to the arrival of the internet, the average age for the exposure to pornography was between the ages of 11 to 13. Now, some researchers state it is down to age 8. In fact, ninety percent of students aged 8—16 have viewed pornography on the internet.[1] The largest group of viewers of internet pornography are children ages 12—17.[2] Children and youth often are introduced to pornography unintentionally by stumbling across its path in some form. To know that children on the internet are only 2 *Clicks* away from seeing pornography accidentally or purposefully is really scary and alarming.

> Eyes so young, so full of pain and stain,
> Cry out for escape from porn's shackling chain.
> Parents, ministers, therapists and friends alike
> Must free them from their awful plight.

This small book is designed for young children. A sequel, *The Poison of Pornography*, is written for older children and young adults. I am indebted to Dr. Timothy Faulk, a clinical counseling therapist, for encouraging the writing of both. Parents and custodians of children are asked to prayerfully determine when each book is appropriate to share with the children under their care.

The actual word *pornography* is used only once in this book (outside this preface). In its place the name *Bad Pictures* is used for clarity.

A television advertisement several decades ago said, "Knowledge is power." And for a truth it is. Knowledge about pornography, even in its simplest and elementary stage, empowers children to reject its deadly, destructive poison. It is my deepest hope that this book will empower children with just enough knowledge about pornography to do that for them.

Parents, grandparents and custodians of young children can prepare them, without scaring them, for encounters with pornography.

In warning young children of pornography, the degree to which it is done is all-important. Parents and authors alike must avoid "overload" of sharing too much too soon and showing insensitivity to a child's emotional and spiritual state by being too detailed and graphic. This is a daunting and difficult challenge but one that must be attempted for the child's sake.

Likewise, the manner in which it is discussed is vital. Make your child feel comfortable in talking with you about sexual issues. Such openness will provide opportunities to steer the child in the right way. Two keys to developing such an "open" relationship is never to show shock or anger to the child with regard to what he or she shares, and never to seek to combat the porn problem through the use of shame or belittlement, which is not only insensitive and ineffective but also injurious to them.

Listen calmly, ask questions gently and give assurance of your love and support. Talk about what might be done so that the viewing of Bad Pictures may never happen again (accidentally or otherwise).

When children are uncomfortable talking about their "porn" experience with you, it is nonetheless expedient for their wellbeing that you lovingly and gently insist.

An ounce of prevention is worth a pound of cure. Protection from the harm that pornography brings to children's lives is worth the time, cost and effort spent by parents in monitoring what they are exposed to by way of the computer, television and cell phone. A possible help in this monitoring is the installation of a porn blocker program on computers in the home, such as *Forcefield*, the preferred parental control software solution of Focus on the Family (http://fotf.forcefield.me).

Pray that God will use this book to protect every child that reads it from pornography's destructive snare, mentally, emotionally, physically and spiritually.

It is a winnable battle.

1

A Big Word with a Bad Meaning

Pornography is a big word that is used to describe Bad Pictures. It will not be used again in this book.

The name Bad Pictures will be used in its place. Bad Pictures are pictures and movies that show people with little or no clothes on.

Bad Pictures show up in many different ways and places, like on the computer, television, cell phone and in magazines and movie theaters.

Sometimes they are shared by a friend or stranger.
Sometimes they are seen accidentally.
But mostly they are seen on purpose.

No matter how or from whom Bad Pictures come,
always turn away from looking at them.

A No Dumping Allowed sign tells people not to dump
trash in the beautiful yard where it is posted.

Hang that sign on
your beautiful life.
It will keep the
ugly trash of
Bad Pictures
out that the
Devil wants
to get in.

2

Bad Pictures Go against What God Says

In the Garden of Eden, Satan told Adam and Eve a lie. He said that it was okay to eat of the fruit. They believed him, ate of it and got hurt. You can read the story in Genesis 3:1–7.

Satan is still telling lies trying to get boys and girls to do what God said was wrong, like looking at Bad Pictures. He tells them that these kinds of pictures are okay, when God says they are not.

And when children listen to Satan's lies, they always get hurt just like Adam and Eve did.

God wants you to be pure and clean on the inside. He says, **"Happy are the pure in heart"** (Matthew 5:8 GNT). To be pure and clean in your heart means not to do anything or look at anything that is wrong or bad (sin).

To look at the filth of Bad Pictures will make that impossible, for it colors the heart with its ugliness and blackness.

The Royal Ambassador pledge that I memorized as a child in part says:

As a Royal Ambassador I will do my best:

To keep myself clean and healthy,
in mind and body.

Make that the motto (goal or aim) of your life. It will protect you from getting hurt with Bad Pictures and other things.

3

Garbage In, Garbage Out

"Garbage in, garbage out" means that the bad stuff looked at or thought about has the power to shape all of your life for the bad.

If you feed your brain with the trash of Bad Pictures, that bad trash will come out in your conduct (behavior).

Oh, be careful little eyes what you see;

Oh, be careful little eyes what you see,

For the Father up above

Is looking down in love.

Oh, be careful little eyes what you see.

The opposite of the chapter title is also true—goodness in, goodness out.

How? The Bible says, "Fill your minds with those things that are good and that deserve praise: things that are true, noble, right, pure, lovely, and honorable" (Philippians 4:8 GNT).

And when you do that, then goodness will come out of your life. It will keep your life beautifully clean inside and out.

4

The Eyes Are Like a Camera

Your eyes are like a camera (just better) that takes pictures and movies. These images are stored in the brain. Unlike those made with a camera, the pictures and movies seen with the eyes are hard to erase (forget).

You cannot "unsee" what is seen. So be careful what you see. Pray with David, saying,

> "Jesus, 'don't let me look at
> worthless [bad] things'"

(Psalm 119:37 ERV).

Children need help to forget the bad, ugly pictures and movies they see. Sometimes they see them out of desire (want to), sometimes by accident, sometimes because they are shown to them by others.

So, should you see Bad Pictures for any of those reasons, it's okay to tell your parents, even if an adult or friend tells you not to.

Your parents understand things like this and want to help you.

5

Don't Explore Bad Pictures

Sometimes friends may want you to explore Bad Pictures with them. Don't do it. It is not necessary.

The Bible says not to give place to such things (Romans 13:14). That is, don't look at Bad Pictures or even think about them. Don't let anybody else make you look at them.

The Apostle Paul says,

"Turn away
     from the
sinful things
     young
       people
want to do.
     Go after
what is right"
(2 Timothy 2:22 NLV).

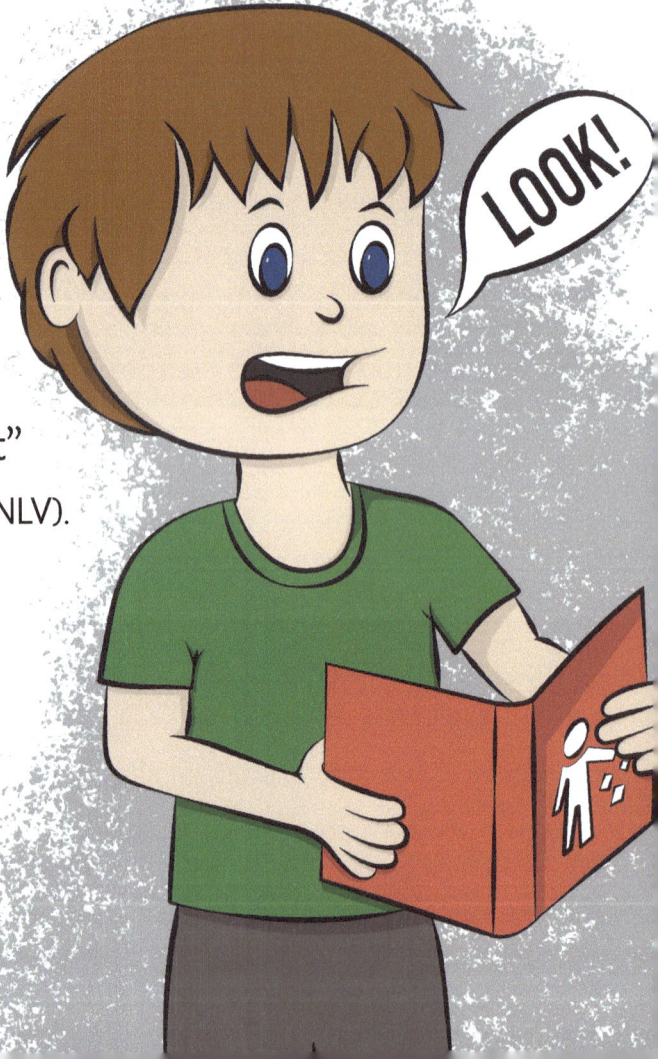

LOOK!

At the first sight of Bad Pictures, turn and run.

You don't have to get into a trash can to know that it contains only stinking trash.

Just so, you don't have to look at Bad Pictures to learn that they are ugly, nasty (unholy), improper, unwholesome (impure), harmful and disgusting (sickening to look at).

So, don't explore Bad Pictures. Just listen to what Jesus, your parents and the pastor say about them.

Let what they say be enough.

6
When Controlled by Bad Pictures

It may take someone only one time looking at Bad Pictures to get to where he doesn't want to stop or feels that he is not able to stop looking at them. These pictures are chained to his life and he cannot get free.

This is called addiction.

Sadly, many people are addicted (chained) to Bad Pictures. They try really hard to stop looking at them but cannot. Bad Pictures control them like alcohol and drugs control people.

And it makes them feel very unhappy.

They need help to stop.

God, parents, ministers and Christian therapists (counselors) can help children stop looking at Bad Pictures. No one with an addiction to Bad Pictures should ever be afraid to ask for help.

God can turn losers into winners. With Paul, those addicted to Bad Pictures may say,

> "I am grateful that God always
>   makes it possible for Christ
>   to lead us to victory"

(2 Corinthians 2:14 CEV).

7

Don't Let Bad Pictures
Live in Your Head

Don't give place to the Devil in your head (thoughts) by thinking about Bad Pictures (Ephesians 4:27). Give the Devil an inch into your life through Bad Pictures and he will take a mile.

When bad thoughts come into your head, talk to Jesus. Read the Bible. Go outside and play. Play a Christian song.

Good thoughts drive out bad thoughts.

The Bible says that we should wear the helmet of salvation.

Roman soldiers wore a helmet to keep their head from injury.

The helmet for Christians is knowing Jesus as Lord and Savior and staying very close to Him. This will help keep their mind or thoughts clean.

You can read about the helmet in Ephesians 6:17.

The Bible also says,

> "Above all else, guard your heart [head], for everything you do flows from it" (Proverbs 4:23 NIV).

Make every effort to keep bad thoughts from entering into your head.

But if they do, don't let them stay.

Tell the ugly thoughts to go back to the Devil who sent them.

Ephesians 6:17

8

The Problem with Bad Pictures Will Not Just Go Away

I hope that you don't have and never will have a problem with looking at bad, ugly pictures. But some children do. And most of the time it's not their fault.

The Devil wants children that have this problem to believe that in time the urge or desire to look at Bad Pictures will just go away, that they will wake up one day never wanting to look at them again.

But they are wrong to think that way.

The truth is that without help now, the problem with Bad Pictures only gets bigger and bigger, worse and worse later.

It simply will not go away on its own.

So get help today if you look at Bad Pictures.

It will be easier to stop now than it will be later.

WORSE

9

I Think I Can; I Know I Can

You have read the story about the "Little Engine That Thought It Could."

Other "engines" refused to even try to pull the heavy train up the big hill. But the Little Engine believed all the time that it could—
and it did.

To stop looking at Bad Pictures is a big, big hill to climb.

But you can do it.

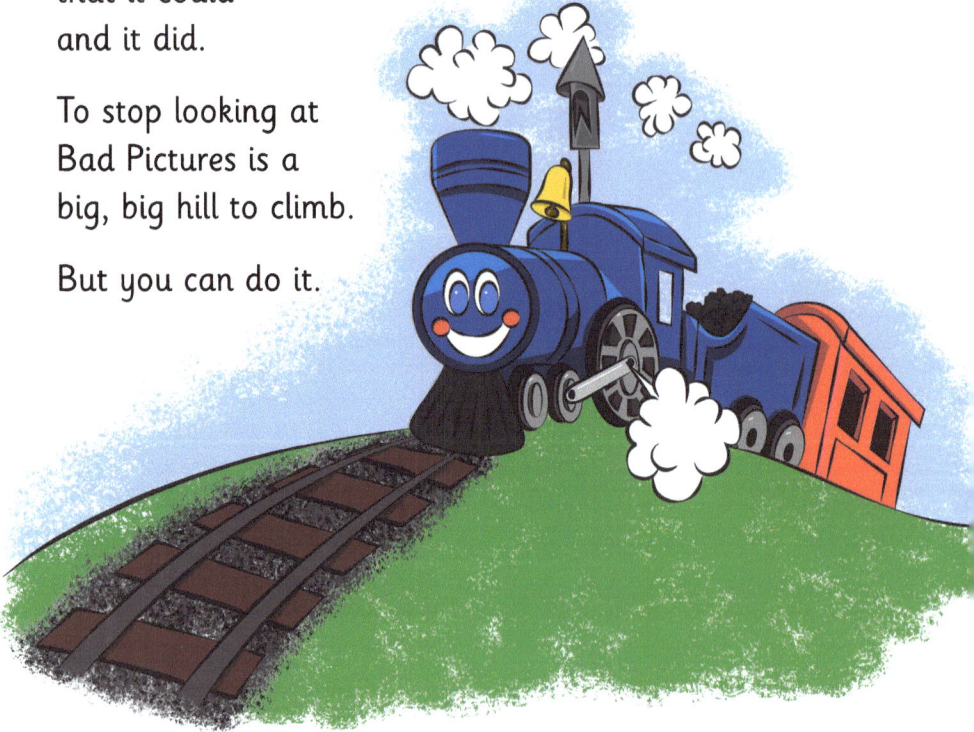

And once you reach the top of the big hill (when you stop looking at Bad Pictures), you will sing in victory with the Little Engine, "I thought I could. I thought I could. I thought I could."

Never say, "I can't"; instead, say,

> "I can do all things through Christ
> who gives me strength"

(Philippians 4:13 BSB).

Jesus said,

"So if the son sets you free,
you will be really free"
(John 8:36 NET Bible).

Bad Pictures mentally (in the head) chain (shackle) you to its ugly and harmful stuff. And the chains are big, heavy and strong, too strong for you to break.

The Bible says in 1 John 4:4 that there is someone that lives in your heart that is greater than the Devil, who can break the chains of Bad Pictures.

That person is Jesus Christ. The Devil has super-strength but Jesus has super-duper-strength.

10

Jesus Loves You When You Are Good or Bad

He loves all the children of the world and wants to forgive them for the bad things they do—like looking at Bad Pictures.

Jesus loves me, He who died
Heaven's gate to open wide;
He will wash away my sin,
Let His little child come in.

~ Anna Bartlett Warner (1859)

When you do something bad (sin), it makes Jesus sad. But it does not keep Him from loving you. After looking at Bad Pictures, a child should right away ask Jesus for forgiveness.

He says,

"And I will forgive the wrongs
they have done,
and I will not
remember their sins"

(Hebrews 8:12 ERV).

Jesus will always forgive when
He is asked to do so.

The Bible says,

"If we confess our sins to God,
He can always be trusted to forgive
us and take our sins away"

(1 John 1:9 CEV).

The word "confess" means "admit." Own up to Jesus
when you look at Bad Pictures.

Tell Him not only that you looked at them but that
you are sorry you did—and He will forgive you.

11

To Change Is to Choose to Change

Yes, Jesus can free children from the control of Bad Pictures.

But first they must want to be freed. Only they can decide (want) this, not their parents or pastor for them.

To change means to choose to let Jesus change you (allow Him to).

And when that choice is made, He will.

Jesus changes a child from the inside out, by forgiving the wrong (sin) he has done, by taking control of his life, and by helping him not to do the same thing again—like looking at bad pictures.

Jesus will this do for everyone who asks, even you. Here is a simple prayer to pray if you ever look at Bad Pictures.

Lord Jesus,
I am sorry that I looked at Bad
Pictures. Forgive me. Help me to
not ever again look at them.
Thank you. Amen.

12

To Look at Bad Pictures or Not?

Looking at Bad Pictures or not is a choice.
The best choice is not to look at them.

The choice is yours to make.

Hopefully you will say:

Bad Pictures my eyes won't see;
I don't want their trash inside of me.

When to me they are shown,
To my parents it will be made known.

There's no need them to explore;
To do so only opens up their ugly door.

Far from Bad Pictures I will stay,
Refusing them the
chance my life to
slay (hurt).

Always I will
pray

Lord Jesus,
keep me from
Bad Pictures'
harmful ways.

Make a pledge (promise, agreement) now like David, who said, 'I will not look at anything that is bad' (Psalm 101:3).

Eyes that don't look at bad pictures can see how wonderful Jesus is and the awesome stuff He has in store for their life. Read Matthew 5:8.

In making the right choice not to look at Bad Pictures, tell your parents and Christian friends. They will help you not to look at them.

Parents, ministers, therapists and friends alike
Are used by God to protect from
Bad Pictures poisonous bite.
Let them help you when in need,
And over porn's temptation you will succeed.

[1] Pornography Statistics. www.familysafemedia.com/pornography_statistics.html, accessed October 17, 2011.
[2] Internet Statistics. https://www.guardchild.com/statistics/, accessed February 21, 2019.

www.ingramcontent.com/pod-product-compliance
Lightning Source LLC
Chambersburg PA
CBHW040035110426
42741CB00030B/28